THE LITTLE HOUSE

By Coningsby Dawson

ISBN - 978-93-5478-715-7

Design and setting By
Zinc Read
Email- zincread@gmail.com

CHAPTER I

HE little house, tell this story. It was lived within my walls; not a line is invented and it was I, by my interfering, who brought about the happy ending. Who wants a story that does not end happily, especially a Christmas story? To have been responsible for the happy ending is pretty nearly as clever as to have made the story up out of one's own head or, as we houses say, out of one's own walls.

Perhaps you never heard before of a house telling a story. If that be so, it is because you don't listen or because you go to bed too early. Unlike people, we houses sleep all day long; but after midnight we wake up and talk. When the clock strikes twelve, our stairs begin to crack and our windows to rattle and our floors to creak. If you ever hear these sounds, don't be frightened; they simply mean that the kind old walls that shelter you have begun to remember and to think. And we have so many things to remember and to think about, especially we old houses who have been standing for almost two hundred years. We have seen so much; we have been the friends of so many generations. More little children have been born beneath our roofs than we have stairs on which to count. We reckon things on our stairs, just as people reckon things on their fingers. When our stairs crack after midnight, it's usually because we're counting' the births and love-makings and marriages we have watched. We very often get them wrong because there are so many of them. Then the doors and windows and floors will chip in to correct us. "Ha," a window will rattle, "you've forgotten the little girl who used to gaze through my panes in 1760 or thereabouts." One of the doors will swing slowly on its hinges and, if anyone disputes with it, will bang, shouting angrily, "Wrong again—all wrong." Then the walls and the windows and the doors and the floors all start whispering, trying to add up correctly the joys and sorrows they have witnessed in the years beyond recall.

" We mutter among ourselves . . . beneath the starlight"

When that happens, if you're awake and listening, you'll hear us start adding afresh, from the lowest to the topmost stair.

I am a London house and a very little house, standing in a fashionable square near Hyde Park. I have known my ups and downs. Once was the time when I was almost in the country and the link-boys used to make a fuss at having to escort my lady so far in her sedan-chair. It's a long way to the country now, for the city has spread out miles beyond me. Within sight through the trees at the end of the square red motor-buses pass, bumping their way rowdily down to Hammersmith and Kew. In my young days these places were villages, but I am told they are full of noises now. I have at least escaped that, for our square is a backwater of quiet and leads to nowhere, having an entrance only at one end. All the houses in the square were built at the same time as I was, which makes things companionable. We all look very much alike, with tiny areas, three stone steps leading up from the pavement, one window blinking out from the ground-floor, two blinking out from each of the other floors and a verandah running straight across us. In summer-time the verandah is gay with flowers. Our only difference is the colour we are painted, especially the colour of our doors. Mine is white; but some of our neighbours' are blue, some green, some red. We're very proud of the front-doors in our square. In the middle stands a railed-in garden, to which none but our owners have access. Its trees are as ancient as ourselves. Behind us, so hidden that it is almost forgotten, stands the grey parish-church, surrounded by a graveyard in which many of the people who have been merry in us rest.

For some years we were what is known as a “gone down neighborhood,” till a gentleman who writes books bought us cheap, put us in repair and rented us to his friends. This has made us very select; since then we have become again fashionable.

Now you know all that is necessary to form a mental picture of us. Because we are so small, we are sometimes spoken of as “Dolls' House Square.” All the things that I shall tell you I do not pretend to have witnessed, for houses have to spend their lives always in the one place—they cannot ride in taxis and move about. We gain our knowledge of how the world is changing by listening to the conversations of people who inhabit us; when night has fallen we mutter among ourselves, passing on to one another beneath the starlight down the lamp-lit streets the gossip we have overheard. Whatever of importance we miss, the churchbells tell us. Big Ben, with his sweet tenor voice, booming out the hours, is in this respect particularly thoughtful.

"*Big Ben, with his sweet tenor voice booming out the hours*"

So now, having explained myself, I come to my story of the little lady who needed to be loved, but did not know it, and the wounded officer who wanted rest.

CHAPTER II

HE little lady who needed to be loved, but did not know it, discovered me quite by accident. This story is a series of accidents; if it had not been for the *ifs* and the *perhaps's* and the *possibilities* there wouldn't have been any story to tell.

I was empty when she found me, for my late tenants had grown frightened and had moved into the country on account of airraids. They said that I was too near the giant searchlights and anti-aircraft guns of Hyde Park Corner to be healthy. If they weren't killed by bombs, sooner or later they would be struck by our own expended shell-cases that came toppling from two miles out of the clouds. So they had made their exit hurriedly in November, taking all their furniture and leaving me to spend my one-hundred-and-ninety-eighth Christmas in the company of a caretaker.

It was shortly before Christmas when I first saw her. Night had settled peacefully down; it was about nine o'clock when the maroons and sirens began to give warning that the enemy was approaching. In an instant, like a lamp extinguished, the lights of London flickered and sank. Down the forests of streets innumerable doors swiftly opened and people came pattering out. Dragging half-clad children by the hand and carrying babies snatched up from their warm beds, they commenced to run hither and thither, seeking the faint red lights of shelters, where cellars and overhead protection might be found. Policemen, mounted on bicycles, rode up and down the thoroughfares, blowing whistles. Ambulances dashed by, tooting horns and clanging bells. From far and near out of the swamp of darkness rose a medley of panic and sound. Prodding the sky, like detectives with lanterns, searchlights hunted and turned back the edges of the clouds. Then ominously, with solemn anger, the guns opened up and in fierce defiance the first bomb fell. The pattering of feet ceased suddenly. Streets grew forlorn and empty. The commotion of living and the terror of dying were transferred from the earth to the air.

I was standing deserted with my door wide open, for at the first signs of clamour the old woman, who was supposed to take care of me, had hobbled up from her basement and out on to the pavement in search of the nearest Tube Station. In her fear for her safety, she had forgotten to close my door, so there I stood with the damp air drifting into my hall, at the mercy of any chance vagrant.

The guns had been booming for perhaps five minutes when I heard running footsteps entering the square. Our square is so shut in and small that it echoes like a church; every sound is startling and can be heard in every part of it. I could not see to whom the footsteps belonged on account of the trees and the darkness. They entered on the side farthest from me, from the street where the red motor-buses pass. When they had reached the top, from which there is no exit, they hesitated; then came hurrying back along the side on which they would have to pass me. *Tip-a-tap, tip-a-tap, tip-a-tap* and panting breath—the sound of a woman's high-heeled shoes against the pavement. Accompanying the *tip-a-tap* were funny, more frequent, shuffling noises, indistinct and confused. Three shadows grew out of the gloom, a small one on either side and a bigger one in the centre; as they drew near they resolved themselves into a lady in an evening-wrap and two children.

I was more glad than I cared to own, for I'd been feeling lonely. Now that peace has come and we've won the war, I don't mind acknowledging that I'd been feeling frightened; at the time I wouldn't have confessed it for the world lest the Huns should have got to know it. We London houses, trying to live up to the example of our soldiers, always pretended that we liked the excitement of airraids. We didn't really; we quaked in all our bricks and mortar. One's foundations aren't what they were when one is a hundred-and-ninety-eight years old. So I'm not ashamed to tell you that I was delighted when the lady and her children came in my direction. I tried to push my front-door wider that they might guess that they were welcome. I was terribly nervous that they might pass in their haste without seeing that I was anxious to give them shelter. It was shelter that they were looking for. In coming into the square they had been seeking a shortcut home.

They drew level without slackening their steps and had almost gone by me when, less than a quarter of a mile away, a bomb crashed deafeningly. Everything seemed to reel. Far and near you could hear the tinkling of splintered glass. The world leapt up red for a handful of seconds as though the door of a gigantic furnace had been flung open. Against the glow you could see the crouching roofs of houses, the crooked chimney-pots and the net-work of trees in the garden with their branches stripped and bare. The lady clutched at my railings to steady herself. Her face was white and her eyes were dark with terror. The last bomb had been so very close that it seemed as though the next must fall in the square itself. One of the searchlights had spotted the enemy and was following his plane through the clouds, holding it in its glare.

"Mummy, it's all right. Don't be frightened. You've got me to take care of you." It was the little boy speaking. Then he saw my *To Let* sign above and pointed, "We'll go in here till it's over. Look, the door's wide open."

He tugged on her hand. With her arm about the shoulder of the little girl on the other side of her, she followed. The glow died down and faded. Soon the square was as secret and shadowy as it had been before—a tank full of darkness in which nothing stirred.

CHAPTER III

EVER since I had been built had any visit quite as unceremonious as this occurred. Who was the strange lady?

What was she doing wandering the streets at this hour unescorted? She was beautiful and richly gowned; her face was young, but very sad. I was anxious to learn more, so I listened intently.

At first on entering, they halted just across the threshold, huddled together, the little lady with an arm flung about each of the children. She seemed to think that someone might be hidden in the darkness watching—someone to whom I belonged—for presently she addressed that supposed someone tremblingly: “We hope you don't mind, but the car forgot to come for us. Grandfather had been giving us a party. When we heard the warning, we tried to run home before the raid started; but we got lost. The Tube Stations were all so crowded that... And we found your door open, so we hope you don't mind us entering.”

She paused nervously, waiting for someone to answer. A board creaked; apart from that the silence was unbroken.

Speaking to herself more than to the children, “It's quite empty,” she said at last.

“Shall I close the door, Mumsie?” the little boy questioned.

“No, Robbie darling,” she whispered; “they might be angry, when they come back. I mean the people who live here.”

“But it's dreadfully cold.”

“Then let's go farther in and find somewhere to sit down till the raid is over.” They stumbled their way in the darkness through the hall and up the narrow staircase, where only one can walk abreast. Robbie went first on this voyage of discovery; he felt that if anything were hiding from them, his body would form a protection. His mother didn't want to lose sight of the street by climbing higher, but he coaxed her on from stair to stair. As pioneer of the expedition, he reached the tiny landing with the single door, which gives entrance to the drawing-room which occupies the whole of the second storey.

Turning the handle he peeped in warily. Then, "Cheer up, Mummy," he cried, "there's been a fire and there's a wee bit of it still burning."

The room was carpetless and bare of furniture, save for an old sofa with sagging springs that had been pulled up across the hearth. Perched on the bars of the grate sat a tin kettle, gasping feebly, with nearly all its water boiled away. Under the kettle a few coals glowed faintly and a weak flame jumped and sank, like a ghost trying to make up its mind to vanish. Through the tall French windows that opened on to the verandah one could see the sky lit up with the tumultuous display of monstrous fireworks. From high overhead, above the clatter of destruction and the banging of guns, came the long-drawn, contented humming of the planes.

"They're right over us," the little boy whispered.

As if afraid that any movement on their part would draw the enemy's attention, they stood silent, clinging together, and listened. Oblongs of light, falling through the windows, danced and shifted. Once the beam of a searchlight groping through the shadows, gazed straight in and dwelt on them astounded, as if to say, "Well, I never! Who'd have thought to find you here?"

They tiptoed over to the couch and sat down, making as little noise as possible, for they still weren't sure that they were welcome. They didn't speak or move for some time; with the excitement and running and losing their way they were very tired. Presently the little boy got up, and went and stood by the window looking out, with his legs astraddle and his hands behind his back like a man. He wore a sailor-suit and had bare, sturdy knees. He was very small to try to be so manly.

"The little boy stood by the window with his legs astraddle"

"I'm not frightened, Mummy," he said.

"If father were here, he wouldn't be frightened."

She shifted her position so that she could glance proudly back at him. "Father was never frightened."

For the first time the little girl spoke. "If father were here, they wouldn't dare to come to London. I expect they knew..."

"Yes, Joan," her mother interrupted quickly, "I expect they knew."

"And when I'm a man they won't dare to come to London, either," said Robbie. "How many of them did father...?"

But at that moment, before he could finish his question, his mother pressed her finger against his lips warningly. Above the roar of what was going on in the clouds, she had heard another and more alarming sound; the front-door closed quietly, a match struck and then the slow deliberate tread of someone groping up the stairs.

CHAPTER IV

HE tread reached the landing and proceeded to mount higher. Then it hesitated. Another match was struck and it commenced to descend. On arriving at the landing again, it halted uncertain. The handle of the door was tried. The door swung open and a man peered across the threshold. No one spoke. The little lady on the couch drew Joan closer to her side and held her breath, hoping that the man might not observe them and that, when he had gone, they might escape. But the man did not go, he stood there on the alert, listening and searching the darkness.

It was Robbie who spoke first. He had thrust his hands deep into his knickerbockers' pockets to gain courage. "What do you want? We think you might speak," he said.

The man laughed pleasantly. "I'm sorry if I've frightened you. I didn't know that anyone was here. I thought this was an empty house. Perhaps you weren't aware of it, but you'd left your front-door open." Then, because no one replied, he added, "It's all right now; it's closed."

He wasn't looking at Robbie any longer. He was trying to probe the shadows by the fireplace, where he had caught the rustle of a woman's dress. He had caught something else—the faint sweet fragrance of Jacqueminot.

"I've alarmed you," he said. "I'm a stranger in London and I couldn't find any way out of your square. I strayed into your house for shelter. I'm sorry I intruded. Good-night to you all, however many there are of you."

He was actually going. It was impossible to see what he looked like, but he was evidently well-mannered and a gentleman. Suddenly to the lady in the lonely house, from being a creature of dread, he became a heaven-sent protector. Who could tell how many less desirable visitors might not call before the raid was ended? The care-taker might return. Were that to happen, it would be much more comfortable to have this male trespasser present to help make the explanations. Just as he was withdrawing, the lady rose from the shabby couch and called him back.

"Oh, please, we'd much rather you didn't go."

"But who are we?"

"I and Robbie and Joan. We did the same thing as you. The house doesn't belong to us. We got caught, just as you did. We were terribly scared and... and it's creepy being in an empty, strange house where you haven't any right to be."

Though she could only see the blur of him, she could feel the smile that was in his eyes when she had finished her appeal. And it was an appeal, eager and nervous and tremulous. The tears in her voice said much more than the words. As he turned on his heel, she heard the jingle of his spurs and guessed that he was a man in khaki.

"I'm on my way to France," he said, speaking slowly; "I only landed yesterday. I was lonely too; I didn't know a soul. A queer way to make a friend!"

As he stepped into the room, the light from the windows fell on him; he was dressed in the uniform of an American officer.

"Which are you?" he asked. "I've heard only your voice as yet. I'll do anything I can to help."

The little lady held out her hand, but her face was still in shadow. It was a very tiny hand. "It's good of you to be willing to stay with us," she said gratefully.

At that point their conversation languished. The circumstances were so unprecedented that they were at a loss what to say or how to act. It was he who broke the awkward silence: "We ought to be able to rouse this fire with a little effort." He bent over it, trying to pull it together. "We need more coal. If you'll excuse me and won't be frightened while I'm gone, I'll run down and see what I can forage."

It seemed a long time that he was gone—so long that she had begun to be afraid that he'd taken his chance to slip out. She wouldn't have blamed him. In the last two years, since she'd been by herself, she'd become used to men doing things like that. She had ceased to bank overmuch on masculine chivalry. Few men had leisure to expend on a woman, however charming and beautiful, whose children had always to be included in the friendship.

When she had made quite sure that he was no more chivalrous than other men, she heard him laboriously returning. He came in carrying a scuttle in one hand and some bundles of wood in the other. "And now we'll pull down the blinds," he said, "and make a blaze and get her going."

On his knees before the hearth he started to work, ramming paper between the bars, piling sticks criss-cross and using his cheeks as bellows. In the intervals between his exertions he chatted, "I'm no great shakes at house-work. You mustn't watch me too closely or laugh at me. I'll do better than this when I've been at the Front, I guess. Are these your kiddies?... I suppose your husband's over there, where I'm going?"

"He was."

"Oh, so you've got him back! You're lucky. Is he wounded or has he got a staff job in England?"

"He'll never come back."

He paused in what he was doing and sat gazing into the flames which were licking at the wood. He hung his head. He ought to have thought of that; in the last few years so many Englishmen were dead. And then there came another reflection—the picture of what it must have cost her husband to say good-bye to his wife and children, and go marching away to anonymous glory. He wasn't married himself, but if he had been... It took enough bolstering up of one's courage to go when one was single; but to go when one was married... And yet selfishly, ever since he had put on khaki his paramount regret had been that, were he to peg out, he would leave no one to carry on in his stead. This air-raid was his first remote taste of warfare; within the next few weeks he was to know it in its full fury. What had impressed him most was the difference between war as imagined and witnessed. As imagined it had seemed the most immense of sports; as witnessed it was merely murder. Just before he had sought shelter he had seen where a bomb had fallen. People had been killed—people not so different from the mother and children hiding in this house. The suddenness of extinction had made him feel that in the game of life he had somehow "missed out." There would be no woman to think of him as "her man" were he to go west. And here was the woman's price for such caring, "He'll never come back."

He turned his head slowly; by the light of the crackling wood for the first time he saw her. The little boy was lying wearied out, with his head bowed in her lap. The little girl sat drowsing against her shoulder.

She herself was leaning forward, gazing at and beyond him with a curious air of resigned intensity. She seemed to him to be listening for someone, whom she knew in her heart was never coming. He noticed the white half-moon of her shoulders faintly showing beneath her chinchilla wrap. He noticed her string of perfect pearls, the single ring on her hand and the expensive simplicity of her velvet gown. He was sufficiently a man of the world to make a guess at her social station. But it wasn't her beauty or elegance that struck him, though they were strangely in contrast to the empty room in which she sat; it was her gentleness and expression of patient courage. He knew, as surely as if she had told him, that this empty room, in which he had found her, was the symbol of her days. It was with her as it was with himself; there was no man to whom she was "his woman."

"I've hurt you by the impertinence of my questions."

She smiled and shook her head. "You've not hurt me. Don't think that. I shouldn't like you to think that you'd hurt me or anything that would make you sad. Are you going to France soon?"

"Tomorrow."

"Then you won't be here for Christmas. I wonder where you'll spend it. Perhaps next Christmas the war will be ended and you'll..." She caught the instant change in his expression. She had seen that look too often in soldiers' eyes when the future was mentioned not to know what it meant. She laid her hand on his arm impulsively. "But everyone who goes doesn't stay there. You'll be one of the lucky ones. You'll come back. I have that feeling about you. I know what's in your mind; you're a long way from home, you're going to face a great danger and you believe that everything is ended. You can only think of war now, but there are so many better things to do with life than fighting. All the better things will be here to welcome you, when you return."

He found himself talking to her in a way in which he had never spoken to any woman. Afterwards, when he recalled their conversation, he wondered why. Was it because she had filled him with so complete a sense of rest? One didn't have to explain things to her; she understood. He asked her how it was that she understood and she replied, "You don't have to go to war to learn how to endure. You can stay at home and yet beat off attacks in the front-line trench. We women defeat despair by keeping on smiling when there's nothing left to smile about, and by wearing pretty dresses when there's no one to take a pride in what we wear."

He retorted unguardedly, as he felt. "But there must be heaps of people who take a pride in you."

"You think so? You're unspoilt and generous. Life's a wonderful dream that lies all before you. You haven't known sorrow. Do you know what you seemed to be saying when you spoke to me through the shadows? 'Everybody has always loved and trusted me, so you love and trust me, too.' If it hadn't been for that, that I saw that you'd always been loved and were lonely for the moment, I shouldn't have sat here talking with you for the last hour. You'll get everything you want from life, if you'll only wait for it. You'll come back."

While he sat at her feet in the firelight, she had the knack of making him feel like a little boy who was being comforted. She kept aloof from him, but she mothered him with words. He found himself glancing up at her furtively to make sure that she wasn't as old as she pretended. She wasn't old at all—not a single day older than himself. He turned over in his mind what she had said about having no one to be proud of her. He would have given a lot for the chance to be proud of her himself. But he was going to France tomorrow—there was no time left for that. With so much fighting and dying to be done, it seemed as though there would never again be time for anything that was personal.

The clamour in the skies had died down.

The crash of guns had been growing infrequent; now it had subsided. The drone of planes could be no more heard. The invader had been driven back; hard on his heels our aerial cavalry were following across the Channel, awaiting their moment to exact revenge when he tried to land.

"*Hard on his heels our aerial cavalry followed him across the Channel*"

The restored normality seemed to rouse her reserve. Lifting the sleeping head from her lap, she whispered, "Wake up, Robbie; we can go home now. It's all over."

The officer had risen and stood leaning against the mantel, "So it's good-bye?"

"I'm afraid so."

"You've made me happy when I least expected to be happy. Shall we meet again, I wonder?"

She smiled at his seriousness. "Perhaps. One never knows what the good God will allow. We didn't expect to meet tonight."

He was sensitive to her evasion and laughed, pretending to make light of it. "We don't want them to think they've had burglars. We had better leave something for the coals we've burned." He placed a pound note on the mantel.

Taking Joan in his arms and going first, he led the way down the stairs. When they were out of the hall and the front-door had closed behind them, he left the little group on the steps and went in search of a taxi. After a lengthy expedition he found one and, by promising an excessive fare, induced the driver to accompany him back. He knew neither the name of the square nor the number of the house, so he had to keep his head out of the window and shout directions. On entering the square he searched the pavement ahead, but could catch no sign of his recent companions. He halted the cab against the curb at the point where he thought he had left them; he was made certain that it was the point when he saw the notice TO LET. Perhaps the caretaker had come back and invited them to enter till he returned. He rang the bell and knocked vigorously. The driver was eyeing him with suspicion. When his repeated knockings were unanswered, he got into the taxi and ordered him to move slowly round the square.

She had completely vanished. Either she had picked up a conveyance for herself, while he had been engaged in his search, or else she had lost faith in him and had taken it for granted that he had deserted her. He did not know her name.

She had given him no address. Tomorrow night he would be in France. He had neither the time nor the necessary information to hunt for her.

In reply to the driver's request for further instructions, he growled the name of his hotel. Then he spread himself out on the cushions and gave way to disconsolate reflections. The night was full of smoke and heavy with the smell of a bonfire burnt out. Things had become again uninteresting. He told himself that the most wonderful hour of his life was ended.

CHAPTER V

HRISTMAS came and went unmerrily. The old woman who took care of me had known better days; she stayed in bed in an effort to forget. Next door, but one, a son had returned unexpectedly from the trenches. There were laughing, dancing and piano playing. I tried to share their happiness; but happiness isn't the same when it is borrowed second-hand. My rooms were cheerless and empty of all sound.

I kept thinking of my air-raid visitors, wondering where they were and hoping that the American officer had re-found the little lady. If he had, I felt sure he would be good to her. I told myself a foolish fairy-story, as old houses will, of how, when the war was ended, they would drive up to my door together, as if by accident, and exclaim, "Why, it's the little house where we first met!" Then the TO LET sign would be taken down and, having fetched Joan and Robbie, we would all live together forever. With luck and love we might have smaller feet to toddle up and down my stairs.

January, February, March commenced and ended, and the TO LET sign was still there. It seemed that nobody would ever want me. It was April now; to their nests in the railed-in garden of the square the last year's birds were coming back. Trees had become a mist of greenness. Tulips and daffodils were shining above the ground. In the window-boxes of other houses geraniums were making a scarlet flare. Without warning the dream, which had been no more than a dream, began to become a fact.

I had been drowsing in the sun, taking no notice of what was happening, when I was suddenly awakened by a sharp rat-a-tat-tat. I came to myself with a start to find that the little lady, unaccompanied, was standing on my steps.

She knocked again and then a third time. There could be no doubt about her determination to enter. At last the old woman heard her and dragged herself complainingly up from the basement. When the door had been narrowly opened, the little lady pushed it wider and stepped smartly into the hall with an exceedingly business-like air. “I have an order from the agents to view the house.”

“I'm 'ard of 'earing. Wot did yer say? Speak louder.”

“I have an order from the agents to look over the house.”

“Let's see your order?”

While the caretaker fumbled for her spectacles, she went on talking. “You won't like it. There's no real sense in your seeing it. It ain't much of a 'ouse—not modern, too little and all stairs.”

It made me furious to hear her running me down and to have no chance to defend myself.

“Nevertheless, I rather like it and I think I'll see it,” the little lady said.

She went from room to room, making notes of the accommodations and thinking aloud as she set them down. “Four floors beside the basement. On the top floor two bedrooms; they'll do for Robbie and Joan and nurse. On the next floor one bedroom and a bathroom; I'll have that for myself. On the second floor one big room, running from front to back; that's where we'II have the parrot and the piano, and where I'll do my sewing. On the ground-floor a dining-room in front and a bedroom at the back; the bedroom at the back will do for cook. I won't have anyone sleeping below-stairs. It's a very wee house, but tremendously cosy. And what pretty views—the garden in the square in front, and the old grey church with its graveyard at the back! It's all so green and quiet, like being in the country.”

"The old grey church with its graveyard at the back"

She had far out-distanced the caretaker, hurrying over the first two floors that she might get to the top by herself. Now, as she descended, she inspected each room more leisurely. As yet she had said no word that would indicate that she had recognised me. I wondered what her motive had been in coming; whether she had deliberately sought me or stumbled on me simply by accident. I would have known her anywhere, though I had been blind and deaf, by the fragrance of Jacqueminot that clung about her.

She had come to the tiny landing on the second floor, when something familiar in her surroundings struck her. She stood there holding the handle of the door and wrinkling her forehead. "It's odd," she whispered; "I can't understand it." She turned the handle and entered. The room smelt stuffy; its windows had not been opened since she was last there. The sunlight, pouring in, revealed motes of dust which rose up dancing every time she stirred. In the grate were the accumulated ashes of many fires. Drawn across the hearth was the shabby couch. Nothing had been altered since she had left it. She passed her hand across her eyes, "It can't be; it would be too strange to find it like that." Then she started to reconstruct the scene as she remembered it. "Robbie was there against the window, asking how many Huns his daddy had brought down, and I was sitting here in the shadow, when quite suddenly we heard his tread on the stairs. The door opened; he said something about being sorry that he'd frightened us, and then.... Why yes, I'm positive." She stepped out onto the verandah and stood looking down into the square. When she turned to re-enter her eyes were moist and shining. "You *are* the little house. Oh, little house, I've dreamt of you so often. Does he dream of you too, where he is out there? Was I right to run away and to doubt him? If you had a tongue you could tell me; did he say hard things about me when he found me gone on coming back?"

CHAPTER VI

WO weeks later they took possession of me. They did it with so much friendliness that at the end of a month it was as though we had always lived together. Even the furniture fitted into all my odd nooks and angles as if it had been made especially for me. And, indeed, it might have been, for most of it was created in the reign of Queen Anne, at which period my walls were, as one might say, feeling their legs. It was very pleasant when night had settled down and everyone was sleeping, to listen to the conversations which were carried on between the new-comers and my own floors and stairs. One grandfather's clock was particularly interesting in his reminiscences. He had told the time to Dr. Johnson and had ticked away the great lexicographer's last hours. On this account he was inclined to be amusingly self-important; it was a permanent source of grievance with him that, so far as the present generation was concerned, his pedigree was unknown. There were times when he would work himself into such passions that his weights would drop with a bang. He was always sorry for it next morning and ashamed to face the little lady. As she came down to breakfast, she would catch sight of his hands and say, "So the poor old clock has stopped again! The old fellow's worn out. We shall have to send him to the mender's."

Perhaps it is hardly fair to repeat this gossip about one piece of the furniture, for everything, myself included, was old; whether we were tables, chairs or stair-cases, we all had our crochets and oddities. But, however much we differed among ourselves, we were united in adoring the youth of the little lady and her children. More than any of us the whispering parrot adored her.

The whispering parrot was a traveller. He had come from Australia fifty years ago.

He played so indispensable a part in producing the happy ending that he deserves an introduction.

He had been the gift of the children's grandfather, a retired General. His plumage was Quaker grey, all except his breast and crest which were a wonderful rose-pink. He had black beady eyes which took in everything; what they saw, he invariably remembered. He had a confidential, hoarse way of speaking, that never rose above a whisper. When you heard him for the first time you supposed that he had a bad sore throat. He had a favorite question which he asked whenever he thought he was not being paid sufficient attention, "What shall we talk about?" He would ask it with his head cocked on one side, while he rubbed his feathers up and down the bars. "What shall we talk about?" he would ask the little lady as she sat sewing beneath the lamp of an evening. She was always by herself when the children had been put to bed. She had no callers and never went anywhere.

"Talk about Polly!" she would say. "I don't know, you good grey bird. Did you think I was lonely? Well, let's see! Who loves Mummy best? Can you answer me that?"

Then he would cock his head still farther on one side and pretend to think furiously. She would have to ask him several times before he would attempt an answer. Usually, when he got ready, he would clear his throat and whisper, "The dustman." After which he would laugh as though his sides were aching: "What a naughty Polly! What a naughty Polly!"

She would maintain a dignified silence till she had emptied her needle. Then she would glance at him reproachfully, "Think again, Mr. Impudence—not the dustman."

So he would think again, and having clambered all over his cage and hung upside down to amuse her, would hazard, "Polly?"

"Not Polly."

Then he would make any number of suggestions, though he knew quite well the answer she required. After each wrong guess he would go off into gales of ghostly merriment. At last he would say very solemnly, “Robbie.”

“Yes, Robbie,” she would reply and scratch his head; after which the game was ended. Soon she would fold away her work, put out the lights and climb the narrow stairs to her quiet bed.

It seemed very sad that, when she was so young, she should have to spend so many hours in talking to a rascally old bird. One can be young for so short a time. How short, those who are old know best.

There were evenings, however, when, after the parrot had answered “Robbie,” she would whisper, “I wonder!” and clasp her hands in her lap, gazing straight before her. On these evenings she would sit very late and would look down at her feet from time to time, as though expecting to see someone crouching there. Taxis would chug their way into the square and draw up at one or other of the dolls' houses. The taxi door would open and after a few seconds close with a bang. There would be the rustle of a woman's dress and the tripping of her slippered feet across the pavement; the bass muttering of her husband paying the driver; laughter; the rattling of a key in the latch; and silence. The little lady would sit quite motionless, listening to the secret homecomings of lovers. Then at last she would nod her head, “You're right, Polly, I expect. There's no one else. No doubt it's Robbie who loves me best.”

CHAPTER VII

UT it wasn't Robbie. The diningroom window was the first to make the discovery. Being on the ground-floor, it gazes across the pavement under the trees and sees many things after nightfall which are missed by the upper storeys. The first and second time that something unusual happened I was not told; not until the third time was I taken into the secret. The dining-room window does most of the watching for the entire house; it sees so much that it has learnt to be discreet.

It was Armistice night when the unusual happening first occurred. London had gone mad with relief from suspense. Wherever a barrel-organ could be found people were dancing. Where more suitable music was not available, tin-cans were being beaten with a dervish, rhythmic monotony. Dance the people must. Their joy had gone into their feet; they could not convince themselves that peace had come till they had danced themselves to a standstill. They invented impromptu steps, dancing twenty abreast in the open spaces, humming any tune that caught their fancy, with their arms linked in those of strangers. But there were no strangers that night; everyone was a friend. Top-hats, evening-dress, corduroys and privates' uniforms hobnobbed together. A mighty roar of laughter and singing went up from thousands of miles of streets, dim-lit and dusk-drenched to ward off the ancient peril from the air. How suddenly unmodern peril had become! All London laughed; all England; all the world. The sound reached the Arctic; polar bears lumbered farther northward, stampeded by the strum of our guffaws. If there were inhabitants on Mars, they must have heard. The war was won. The news was so incredible that we had to make a noise to silence our doubts.

Everything that could rejoice was out under the stars making merry. We had hidden so long, walked so stealthily, wept so quietly, hated so violently that our right to be happy was almost too terrible to bear. We expressed our joy foolishly, hysterically, inadequately by shouting, embracing, climbing lamp-posts, riding on the roofs of taxis. What did it matter so long as we expressed it and brought the amazing truth home to ourselves? The last cannon had roared. The final man had died in battle. The wicked waste of white human bodies was ended. There would be no more rushing for the morning papers and searching the casualty lists with dread; no more rumours of invasions; no more musterings for new offensives. The men whom we loved were safe; they had been reprieved at the eleventh hour. We should have them home presently, seated by their firesides. It seemed like the fulfilment of a prophet's ecstasy; as though sorrow and crying had passed away and forever there would be no death.

There were two people who did not dance, climb lamp-posts, beat tin-cans and ride on the roofs of taxis that night. Perhaps they were the only two in London; they were both in Dolls' House Square. The little lady was one. She had tucked Joan and Robbie safely in their beds. She had kissed them "Good-night" and turned the gas on the landing to a jet. She had gone part way down the narrow stairs and then... and then she had come back. She had picked up Joan and carried her into Robbie's room. When the two heads were lying close together on the pillow, she had seated herself in the darkness beside them.

The little boy stretched up his arms to pull her down; she resisted. His hands wandered over her face and reached her eyes. They were wet. His heart missed a beat. He knew what that meant. So often in the dark, dark night he had wakened with the sure sense that she was crying and had tiptoed down the creaking stairs to creep in beside her and place his small arms tightly about her.

"Never mind; you have me, Mummy." That was what he always said. He whispered it now.

"Yes, I have my wee man."

"And me, Mummy," Joan murmured sleepily.

"Mummy knows. She has you both. Don't worry about her. She's feeling silly tonight."

"Because you're happy?" Joan questioned.

"Yes, happy for so many little boys and girls whose soldier daddies will be coming back to them soon. Don't talk any more. Go sleepy-bye."

But Robbie knew that it wasn't happiness that made her cry; he knew that she was crying because she had no soldier to come back. What could he say to comfort her? His eyes grew drowsy while he thought about it. He waited till Joan was in Sleepy-bye Land, then with an effort he opened his eyes.

"Mummy, do you know what I'd like best for Christmas?"

"I thought you were sleeping. Don't tell me now. There's heaps of time. It's six weeks till Christmas."

"But Joan and I have talked about it," he persisted. "We don't want him, if you don't want him."

"What is he, dear? If he doesn't cost too much, you shall have him."

Robbie procrastinated now that he had brought his mother to the point of listening. It was a delicate proposal that he was about to make. "I don't know whether you can get one," he hesitated. "A boy at my school got one without asking, and it wasn't even Christmas."

He was sitting up in bed now, very intense and serious, and very much awake.

"But you've not told me yet what it is you want. If you don't tell me, I can't say whether I can afford it."

She slipped her arm about the square little body and feeling how it trembled, held it close against her breast. He hid his face in the hollow of her neck. "Robbie's place," she whispered. "If it's difficult to say, whisper it to mother there."

His lips moved several times before a sound came and then, "If it isn't too much trouble, we should like to have a Daddy."

Against his will she held him back from her, trying to see his eyes. "But why?"

It was he who was crying now. "Oh Mummy, I didn't mean to hurt you.... To be like all the other little boys and girls." When at last he was truly asleep and she had come down to the lamp-lit room in which she sewed, she did not take up her work. The parrot tried to draw her into conversation with his eternal question, "What shall we talk about?"

"Nothing tonight, Polly," she said. Presently she crossed the room and, pulling back the curtains, stood staring out into the blackness. So her children had felt it, too—the weight of loneliness! She had tried so hard to prevent them from sharing it; had striven in so many ways to be their companion. Try as she would, she could never make up for a father's absence. She could never give them the sense of security that a man could have given without effort, even though he had loved them less. It was a bitter realisation—one which vaguely she had always dreaded must come to her. It was doubly bitter coming to her now, on a night when all the world was glad. She might be many things to her children; she could never be a man.... What did Robbie think? That you bought a father from an agency or engaged him through an advertisement? She smiled sadly, "Not so easy as that."

"What shall we talk about?" asked the parrot.

She drew the curtains together, extinguished the lights and groped her way up to bed.

But her eyes had not peered far enough into the blackness. There was another person in London who had not danced or climbed lamp-posts or ridden on the roofs of taxis that night. For three hours he had watched the little house from the shadow of the trees across the road. From the pavement, had you been passing, you would hardly have distinguished him as he leant against the garden-railings. The only time he gave a sign of his presence was when the red flare of his cigarette betrayed him. He did not seem to be planning harm to anyone; he could not have done much harm in any case, for the left sleeve of his coat hung empty. He was simply waiting for something that he hoped might happen. At last his patience was rewarded when she drew aside the curtain and stood with the lighted room behind her, staring out into the blackness. Only when she had again hidden herself and all the house was in darkness, did he turn to go. He was there the next night and the next. It was after his third night of watching that the dining-room window told me.

CHAPTER VIII

HE fourth night he was there again. By this time everything in the house, from the kettle in the kitchen to the carpet on the topmost landing, was aware that a one-armed man was hidden beneath the trees across the road, watching. The whole house was on the alert, listening and waiting—everybody, that is to say, except the people most concerned, who inhabited us. It seemed strange that they alone should be in ignorance. The grandfather clock did his best to tell them. "Beware; take care. Beware; take care," he ticked as his pendulum swung to and fro. They stared him in the face and read the time by his hands, but they had no idea what he was saying.

What could it be that the watching man wanted? Whatever it was, he wanted it badly, for it was by no means pleasant to stand motionless for several hours when the November chill was in the air. Nor did he seem to find it pleasant, for every now and then he coughed and shook himself like a dog inside his coat, and sunk his chin deeper into his collar.

He had been there since six o'clock. He had seen the cook and the housemaid come up the area-steps and meet their respective sweethearts under the arc-light at the end of the square. There was only one other grown person in the house beside the little lady—Nurse; and Nurse had been in bed since the afternoon with a sick headache. He could not have known that. It was at precisely eight that he consulted his luminous wrist-watch, crossed the road, hesitated and raised the knocker very determinedly, as if he had only just arrived and had not much time to spare. *Rat-tat-tat!* The sound echoed alarmingly through the silence. The little lady dropped her sewing in her lap and listened. The sound was repeated. *Rat-tat-tat!* It seemed to say, "Come along. Don't keep me waiting. You've got to let me in sooner or later. You know that."

"It can't be the postman at this hour," she murmured, "and yet it sounds like his knock."

Laying her work on the table beneath the lamp, she rose from her chair and descended. She opened the door only a little way at first, just wide enough for her to peer out, so that she could close it again if she saw anything disturbing.

"So you do live here!" The man outside spoke gladly. "I guessed it could be no one else the moment I saw that the house was no longer empty."

She opened the door a few more inches. His tone puzzled her by its familiarity. His face had not yet come into the ray of light which slanted from the hall across the steps.

"You don't recognise me?" he questioned. "I called to let you know that I did fetch that taxi. It's been on my mind that you thought I deserted you. Taxi-cabs were hard to find in an air-raid."

She flung the door wide. "Why it's——"

She didn't know how to call him—how to put what he was into words. He had been simply "the American officer"—that was how she had named him in talking with the children. He had been often remembered, especially during the fireside hour when in imaginary adventures he had been the hero of many stories. How brave she had made him and how often she had feared that he was dead! There were other stories which she had told only to herself, when the children were asleep and the house was silent. And there he stood on the threshold, with the same gallant bearing and the same eager smile playing about his mouth. "I've always been loved and trusted; you love and trust me, too"—that was what his smile was saying to her.

Her heart was beating wildly; but nothing of what she felt expressed itself in what she said. "I'm by myself. I've let the maids go out. I'm terribly apologetic for having treated you so suspiciously."

He laughed and stepped into the hall. "I seem fated to find you by yourself; you were alone last time. I'm in hospital and have to be back by ten. Won't you let me sit with you for half an hour?"

He had begun to remove his top-coat awkwardly. His awkwardness attracted her attention.

"Please let me do that for you."

"Oh, I'm learning to manage. It's all right.... Well, if you must. Thanks." She didn't dare trust herself. There was a pricking sensation behind her eyes. She motioned to him to go first. As she followed him up the stairs, she gazed fixedly at his flattened left side, where the sleeve was tucked limply into the tunic-pocket. She knew that when she was again face to face with him she must pretend not to have noticed.

He entered the room and stood staring round. "The same old room! But it didn't belong to you then. How did you manage it?"

"Easily, but not on purpose."

"Truly, not on purpose?" His tone was disappointed.

"No, not on purpose. I didn't know the name of the square or the number of the house that night. I stumbled on it months later by accident. It was still to let."

"So you took it? Why did you take it?"

"Because I'd liked it from the first and it suited me," she smiled. "Why else?"

"I thought perhaps..."

"Well, say it. You're just like Robbie. When Robbie wants to tell me something that's difficult, he has a special place against which he hides his face; it's easier to tell me there. You men are all such little boys. If it's difficult to tell, you do the same and say it without looking at me."

She reseated herself beneath the lamp and took up her sewing. "Now tell me, why did you want me to say that I took it on purpose?"

"I don't quite know. Perhaps it was because, had I been you, I should have taken it on purpose. One likes to live in places where he has been happy, even though the happiness lasted only for an hour."

He wandered over to the couch before the fire and sat down where he could watch her profile and the slope of her throat beneath the lamp. The only sound was the prick of the needle and the quiet pulling through of the thread. It had all happened just as he would have planned it. He was glad that she was alone. He was glad that it was in this same room that they had met. He was glad in a curious unreasoning way for the faint fragrance of Jacqueminot that surrounded her. It had been just like this at the Front that he had thought of her—thought of her so intensely that he had almost caught the scent and the rustle of her dress, moving towards him through the squalor of the trench. Through all the horror the brief memory of her gentleness had remained with him. And what hopes he had built on that memory! He had told himself that, if he survived, by hook or by crook he would search her out. In hospital, when he had returned to England, all his impatience to get well had been to get to her. In his heart he had never expected success. The task had seemed too stupendous. And now here he was, sitting with her alone, the house all quiet, the fire shining, the lamp making a pool of gold among the shadows, and she, most quiet of all, taking him comfortably for granted and carrying on with her woman's work. At last he was at rest; not in love with her, he told himself, but at rest.

It was she who broke the silence. "How did you know? What made you come so directly to this house?"

He met her eyes and smiled. "Where else was there to come? It was the one place we both knew. I took a chance at it." And then, after a pause, "No, that's not quite true. I was sent up to London for special treatment. The first evening I was allowed out of hospital, I hurried here and, finding that our empty house was occupied, stayed outside to watch it."

"But why to watch it?"

"Because it was a million to one that you weren't the tenant. Before I rang the bell I wanted to make certain. You see I don't know your name; I couldn't ask to see the lady of the house. If she hadn't been you, how could I have explained my intrusion?"

"And then you made certain?"

He nodded. "You came to the window on Armistice night and stood for a few minutes looking out."

"I remember." She shivered as if a cold breath had struck her. "I was feeling stupid and lonely; all the world out there in the darkness seemed so glad. I wish you had rung my bell. That was three nights ago."

"You mean why did I let three nights go by. I guess because I was a coward. I got what we call in America 'cold feet.' I thought..."

He waited for her to prompt him. She sat leaning forward, her hands lying idle in her lap. He noticed, as he had noticed nearly a year ago, the half-moon that her shoulders made in the dimness. She was extraordinarily motionless; her motionlessness gave her an atmosphere of strength. When she moved her gestures said as much as words. Nothing that she did was hurried.

"Tell me what you thought." she said quietly. She spoke to him as she would have spoken to Robbie, making him feel very young and little. When she spoke like that there was not much that he would not have told her.

"I thought that you might not remember me or want to see me. We met so oddly; after the lapse of a year you might easily have regarded my call as an impertinence."

"An impertinence!" There were tears in her eyes when she raised her head. "You lost your arm that I and my children might be safe, and you talk about impertinence."

"Oh, that!" He glanced down at his empty sleeve. "That's nothing. It's the luck of the game and might have happened to anybody."

"But you lost it for me," she re-asserted, "that I might be safe. You must have suffered terribly."

Seeing her distress, he laughed gaily. "Losing an arm wasn't the worst that might have happened. I'm one of the fortunate ones; I'm still above ground. The thing wasn't very painful—nothing is when you've simply got to face it. It's the thinking about pain that hurts.... Hulloa, look at the time; I can just get back to the hospital by ten. If we're late, they punish us by keeping us in next night."

At the top of the stairs as she was seeing him out, he halted and looked back into the room. "It's quiet and cosy in there. I don't want to leave; I feel like a boy being packed off to school. You can't understand how wonderful it is after all the marching and rough times and being cut about to be allowed to sit by a fire with a woman. I loved to watch you at your sewing."

"It's because you're tired," she said, "more tired than you know. You must come very often and rest."

CHAPTER IX

N the weeks that followed the little house came to know him

well. Everybody in the little house treated him as though his injury were a decoration, which had been won especially in their defence. They were prouder to see him come walking up their steps with his blue hospital band on his remaining arm, than if Sir Douglas Haig himself had called upon them. Nobody took any count of the frequency of his visits—nobody except himself. Nobody seemed to think it strange that the moment the doctors had finished his dressings, he should wander off to Dolls' House Square. Nobody seemed to guess just how fond he was of the little lady. He hardly guessed himself. There were times when he wondered exactly how fond he was. He did not believe he was in love with her; the feeling that he had was too gentle. He had always understood that love was exciting, passionate and tumultuous with dreads, whereas in her presence he knew neither fears nor hesitancies. He wasn't the least in terror that he would lose her. He felt simply safe, the way a ship might feel when the winds had ceased to buffet and it lay still in a sheltered harbour on a level keel. This feeling of safety struck him as an extraordinary sensation to be produced in a soldier by a woman; he was a trifle ashamed of it, as though it were not quite manly.

While he spoke with her, he found himself believing with a child-like faith that all women were mothers and that the world was good. He knew that for the present he could not do without her, but he was at a loss to imagine what he would do with her for always. She was like religion—she went beyond him, was bigger and better. He only dimly understood her, but was comfortable in believing that everything hidden was as kind as the part he knew. In a strangely intimate way he worshipped her, as a child adores his mother, thinking her the most perfect and beautiful being in the world. He discovered in her a wisdom of which nothing in her conversation gave the least indication; her unhurried attitude towards life created the impression. If this were love, then all the hearsay information he had gathered on the subject was mistaken.

There were days when, after his wound had been dressed and he had left the hospital, he made a pretence that he was not going to visit her. He told himself that he was making her a habit, and that to make a habit of anyone was foolish. Instead of going to Dolls' House Square, he would invent some urgent business and take himself off citywards. But expeditions in which she had no share soon grew flat. He would find himself thinking about her, wondering whether she was waiting for him. He would end up, as he always ended up, by jumping in a taxi and knocking on her door in Dolls' House Square.

He never once found her out. There was invariably a welcome for him. He would take his seat by the fire in the quiet room and watch her sewing till the darkness deepened and the lamp had to be brought out. It didn't seem to matter much whether he talked or was silent; her contentment seemed complete when he was there. She made no effort to entertain him, which was the best proof of their friendship. She was perfectly willing that he should ignore her, if that was his mood, by reading the paper or playing with the children.

Though she made no effort to entertain him, the entire household had re-organised itself in readiness for his sharp *rat-a-tat*. Everyone, without expressing the fact, recognised that it was nice to have a man about the house. When one rose in the morning, there was something to which to look forward now. A man dropping in, even occasionally, gave this group of women a sense of protection and of contact with the unwidowed world.

To Robbie and Joan he stood for something midway between a big brother and a pal. They had sharp rivalries as to who should light his cigarette. It wasn't easy for him to grip the box between his knees and strike the match with only one hand. They watched him and by anticipating his wishes tried to constitute themselves his missing hand.

When they were with him, the little lady withdrew into the background, making herself so still and self-effacing that it scarcely seemed that he had come to see her. It was as though she had three children; he appeared to be their friend much more than hers. He would carry them off to the Zoo, to matinees or to see the Christmas toys in the West End shops. Sometimes she would accompany them; more often she would listen to their adventures when they had returned. But she never was really left out. While they were absent from her, she formed the main topic of conversation. Of this she was well aware; if she had not been, she would not have been so happy.

In a way she derived more pleasure from staying at home and picturing them laughing through the crowded streets, going into tea-shops, riding in taxis and coming back through the dusk together. The children looked so proud in their sole possession of a man, especially of a soldier who had been wounded. Had their father come through the war, that was how they would have looked in his company. She was glad that they should get away from skirts. He could give them something which it was not in her power to give, however much she loved them. She was only a woman. Her reward followed when they returned a little conscience-stricken at having left her, bringing with them a present as indisputable proof that she had been remembered.

One evening in talking with her after the children had been put to bed, he asked her if she didn't think she ought to go out more often.

"I know I ought."

"Then why don't you?"

She smiled gently, thinking how little he knew of the world. "When you've not got your own man to take you, it's difficult. The world moves in pairs. A woman can't go to many places unaccompanied."

"But surely you don't need to. You must have quantities of friends who would be glad..."

She cut him short. "When a woman is left by herself, she learns a good many things about men that she didn't suspect when she was married. The men she would trust herself with have their wives or fiancées—they have no time to trouble over shipwrecked women like myself. And the other kind of men... The world has no place for a widow. It doesn't mean to be unkind, but it simply doesn't know what to do with her. Unmarried women consider her an unfair rival; they think she's seeking a second chance before they've had their first. In the old days India solved the problem by burying us with our husbands. In England they do the same thing, only less frankly. It's rather stupid to have to live and yet to be treated as though you ought to be dead. One fights against it at first; then one gradually becomes reconciled to be out of the running. If one's wise, she puts all her living into her children."

"But that's not fair," he spoke hotly.

"It's the way it happens."

He sat frowning into the fire. What she had told him had upset all his preconceptions about her. Without looking at her, he re-started the conversation. "I've thought of you as being so happy. I always thought of you that way at the Front. I've pictured you as being perched high on a ledge out of reach of waves and storms. From the first you've given me the feeling that nothing could hurt or move you, and that nothing could hurt or move me while I was near you. It's a queer thing for a man to admit to a woman, but you make me feel absolutely safe."

"That's not so very queer," she said, "because that's the way you make me feel."

"Do I? You're not laughing at me?" He swung round, leaning over the back of the couch, his entire attitude one of amazement.

She met his surprise with a quiet smile. "I'm perfectly serious. But you know the reason why we feel so safe in each other's company? It's because, in our different ways, we're both lonely people. We're not like the rest of the world; we don't move in pairs. I'm lonely because I'm a woman on my own, and you're lonely because you're in hospital in a foreign country. We met just at the time when we could give each other courage."

"But you don't look lonely," he protested; "one always thinks of lonely people as being sad and untidy. You always look so terrifically well-groomed and expensive. You create the impression that you're either going to or returning from a party. I never saw you when you weren't self-assured and occupied. I used to wonder how you spared me so much time from your engagements."

"Clever of me, wasn't it?"

Instead of answering her, he came over and stood above where she sat stitching beneath the lamp. He was seeing her for the first time not as wise, self-reliant and fashionable, but as beautiful, alone and unprotected. He could almost feel the ache of the bruises she had suffered. He felt self-reproached; what had he given her? Up to now anything that he could have given had seemed too small to mention. He had taken from her continually, supposing that she had a surplus of everything. And all the while she had been sharing his own hunger for the presents that money cannot buy.

"It's great to be alive, when you'd expected to be dead."

It was her turn to be surprised. She raised her head quickly, recognising a new earnestness in his tone.

"One doesn't talk much of what happened at the Front"

"One doesn't talk much about what happened at the Front," he said; "but one can't help feeling that his life was spared for some definite purpose. I believe the purpose was to be happy and to make others happy. I don't want to hog my own pleasure any more or to trifle in the old slovenly ways. I want to crowd every second with gratefulness for the mere fact of living. That's what's been bringing me here so often. That's why I've been so glad to carry Joan and Robbie away. Kiddies mean so tremendously much more to me than they did before I nearly died. And then there's home and women. I took them for granted once, but now... It's like saying one's prayers to be in a good woman's presence. I don't know if you at all understand me. I'm trying to thank you for what you've done...."

And there his eloquence failed, leaving him gazing down at her and wondering whether she thought him foolish. She patted his hand, but she did not meet his eyes. "It's all right. Don't explain. I know what you're meaning to say."

"Do you?" He spoke doubtfully. "I think I was trying to ask you if we couldn't be happy together. I'm not married and I'm not engaged; but I'm not like the other men you mentioned."

"My dear boy, I never thought you were. If I had, you wouldn't have been here. You're honourable all the way through; I knew that the moment I saw you. Does that make you feel better?"

He laughed happily. "Much. Do you know what I believe I've been trying to ask you through all this maze of words? If I get permission from the doctor to stay out late tomorrow night, would you be gay and go with me to a theatre?"

Her eyes met his with gladness. "I should love it."

CHAPTER X

HAT evening at the theatre was the first conscious step in their experiment of being happy together. She received word from him at lunch-time that the doctor's permission had been granted and that he would call for her at seven. The news made her as excited as if she had never been to a theatre before in her life. She spent the afternoon before the mirror, brushing and re-brushing her hair, and in laying out all the pretty clothes which she knew men liked. It was three years since she had dressed with the deliberate intent that a man should admire her. Once to do that had been two-thirds of her life. To find herself doing it again seemed like waking from a long illness; she could hardly bring herself to believe that the monotony of sorrow was ended and that she was actually going to be happy again. She had been made to feel so long that to be happy would be disloyalty to past affections.

She locked her bedroom door, for fear any of the servants should guess how she was occupied. She was filled with an exultant shame that she should still be capable of valuing so highly a man's opinion of her appearance. "But I will be happy," she kept telling herself; "I have the right." And then, in a whisper, "Oh, little house, you have been so kind. Wish me luck and say that he'll think me nice."

"In flickering pin-points of incandescence, street-lamps wakened"

Outside in the bare black cradle of the trees the November afternoon faded. Sparrows twittered of how winter was almost come. Against the cold melancholy of the London sky, like silhouettes crayoned on a wall of ice, roofs and chimneys stood smudged. In flickering pin-points of incandescence street-lamps wakened; night came drifting like a ship into harbour under shrouded sails.

She had been sitting listening for a long time, haunted by childish fears that he would not come. At seven promptly a taxi panted into the square and drew up wheezing and coughing before the little house. Seizing her evening-wrap, she ran down the stairs and had her hand on the door before his knock had sounded. "I didn't want to keep you waiting," she explained.

He handed her into the cab. With a groan and a thump the engine pulled itself together and they made good their escape. As she settled back into her corner, pulling on her gloves, she watched him. So he also had regarded it as a gala-night! He was wearing a brand-new uniform and had been at extra pains to make his boots and belt splendid and shiny. She did her best not to be observed too closely, for her eyes were overbright and her color was high. She felt annoyed at herself for being so girlish.

"It's tremendous fun. I haven't been to the theatre in the evening since... for years and years," she whispered. "The war is really ended. I'm believing it for the first time."

They dined together at Prince's to the fierce discords of Jazz music. It suited her mood; it was primitive and reckless. Diners kept rising between courses and slipping out in pairs to where dancing was in progress. The whole world went in pairs tonight. And she had her man; no one could make her lonely for just this one night. It was exciting to her to notice how much more they seemed to belong to each other now that they were in public. He felt it also, for he showed his sense of pride and ownership in a hundred little ways. It was good to be owned after having been left so long discarded. As he faced her across the table, he had the air of believing that everybody was admiring her and envying him his luck. She was immensely grateful that he should think so. It was as though he could hear them saying, "How on earth did a one-armed fellow do it?" Had they asked him, he could only have told them, "The house was empty, so I entered." Yes, and even he had not guessed how empty! But what had changed her? Knowing nothing about the locked door and how her afternoon had been spent, he was puzzled. All he knew was that the woman whom he had thought perfect, had revealed herself as more perfect. She had become radiantly beautiful in a way quite new and unexpected.

Of the play to which they went she saw but little; all she realised was that it was merry—a fairy-tale of life. One does not notice much when the heart is swollen with gladness. People sang, and looked pretty, and fell in love. Everyone was paired and married before the curtain was rung down. Something, however, she did remember: two lilting lines which had been sung:

And, while the sun is shining,
Make hay, little girl, make hay.

They kept repeating themselves inside her head. Unconsciously in the darkness as they were driving home, she started humming them.

"What did you say?" he questioned.

"I didn't say anything. It was just a snatch from a tune we heard."

"Was it? Won't you hum it again?"

So in the intermittent gloom of the passing lights she tried; but for some reason, inexplicable to herself, it made her feel choky. She couldn't reach the end. Gathering her wrap closer about her, she drew the fur collar higher to hide the stupid tears which had forced their way into her eyes.

“I believe you're crying!” he exclaimed with concern. “Do tell me what's the matter.”

“I'm too happy,” she whispered brokenly. The taxi drew up against the pavement with a jerk. There was no knowing what he might say next to comfort her. She both yearned to learn and dreaded. Flight was the safer choice. Before he could assist her, she had jumped out. “Come tomorrow and I'll thank you properly. I can't now. And... I'm sorry for having been a baby.” Catching at her skirts, she fled up the steps and let herself into the darkened house.

Not until his wheels had moved reluctantly away, did she climb the narrow stairs to the room from which she had departed so gaily. Her solitariness had returned. She had had her own man for a handful of hours. They were ended.

As she threw off her finery, she could still hear that voice persistently advising,

And, while the sun is shining,
Make hay, little girl, make hay.

In the darkness she flung herself down on the bed, burying her face in the pillow. “I want to; oh, I want to,” she muttered.

CHAPTER XI

OR three weeks she followed the song's advice. No one knew how long happiness would last. With her it had never lasted. He would leave her presently; already he was anticipating an early return to America.

"I shall feel terribly flat when you've gone," she told him. "But I'll write. I'll write you the longest letters."

"Ah, but letters aren't the same as being together."

He didn't seem to share her need of him, and it hurt. If he did share it, it was unconsciously. He had yet to awaken to what the need meant. She had allowed him to become too sure of her, perhaps; had she kept him more uncertain, he might have awakened. In any case, it was too late to alter attitudes now and to think up reasons.

He liked her in the jolliest kind of way as the most splendid of diversions; but she wasn't essential to him for all time—only for the present. She treasured no illusions about the longest letters. She knew men—the world was filled with women; out of sight would be out of mind. So every evening when he visited her, her heart was in her throat till she had made him confess that he had not yet received his embarkation orders. Some day he would tell her that he was going and would expect her to congratulate him. She would have to smile and pretend that she was glad for his sake. After that he would vanish and the long eventlessness would re-commence. He would write intimately and often at first; little by little new interests would claim him. There would be a blank and then, after a long silence, a printed announcement, curtly stating that he had found his happiness elsewhere.

She saw herself growing old. The children would spring up so quickly. She would be left with her pride, to dress and make herself beautiful for an anonymous someone whose coming was indefinitely postponed. Youth would go from her. For interminable evenings, stretching into decades, she would watch afternoons fade into evenings. Everything would grow quiet. She would sit beneath the lamp at her sewing. The whispering parrot would take pity on her and croak, "What shall we talk about?" Even that game would end one day, for Robbie would become a man and marry. When that had happened it wouldn't be truthful for the parrot to tell her that Robbie loved her best. She would listen for the clock to strike, the fire to rustle, the coals to drop in the grate. Towards midnight taxis would enter the square. Lovers would alight. She would hear the paying of the fare, the tapping of a woman's high-heeled shoes on the pavement, the slipping of the key into the latch, the opening and closing of the door, and then again the silence. She would fold up her work, turn out the lights and stand alone in the darkness, invisible as a ghost.

Ah, but he had not sailed yet. "Make hay, little girl, make hay." His going was still only a threat. There was time, still time. She set a date to her respite. She would not gaze beyond it. If she could only have him till Christmas!

Meanwhile he kept loyally to his contract that they should be happy together. He gave her lavishly of his time. If he guessed how much the gift meant, he said nothing to show it. He was like a great, friendly schoolboy in his cheerfulness; he filled every niche of her desire. Now, in the afternoon, when he took the children on adventures, she found herself included. On the return home, he shared with her the solemn rite of seeing them safely in bed. Then forth they would sally on some fresh excursion. Always and increasingly there was the gnawing knowledge that the end was nearer in sight—that soon to each of the habits they were forming they would have to say, "We have done it for the last time."

We, the bricks and mortar of the little house, watched her. We grew desperate, for we loved her. What we had observed and overheard by day we discussed together by night. If we could prevent it, we were determined that he should not go.

"But, if he goes," creaked the staircase, "he may return. They used to say in my young days that the heart grows fonder through absence."

"Rubbish," banged the door on the first landing. "Rubbish, I say."

"He'll go," ticked the grandfather clock pessimistically. "He'll go. He'll go."

"Not if I know it," shouted the door and banged again.

We had come to a few nights before Christmas. Which night I do not remember, but I recall that we had started our decorations. Mistletoe was hanging in the hall. Holly had been arranged along the tops of the picture-frames. The children had been full of whisperings and secrets. Parcels had already begun to arrive. They were handed in with a crackling of paper and smuggled upstairs to a big cupboard in which they were hidden from prying eyes. The children were now in bed, sleeping quietly for fear of offending Santa Claus. The little lady was in the room where she worked, checking over her list of presents. She had got something for everyone but Robbie; she had postponed buying Robbie's present for a very special reason of which we were all aware. Perhaps it was superstition; perhaps a desperate hope. He had told her what he wanted; it didn't look as if she would be able to get it. "It's no good waiting," she told herself; "I shall have to buy him something tomorrow." Just then, as if in answer to her thoughts, an impatient *rat-tat-tat* resounded. It was his unmistakably, but he had never come so late as this before. All day she had listened and been full of foreboding; she had despaired of his ever coming. There was an interval after the door had been opened, during which he removed his coat. She could picture his awkwardness in doing it. Then the swift, leaping step of him mounting the stairs. Why had he delayed so long, only to come to her at the last moment in such a hurry? She rose from her chair to face him, her hands clenched and her body tense, as if to resist a physical blow. As he appeared in the doorway his lips were smiling. There was evidently something which he was bursting to tell her. On catching sight of her face he halted. His smile faded.

"What's the matter? What's happened?" She unclenched her hands and looked away from him. "Nothing."

"There must be something. Something's troubling you. What have you been doing with yourself this evening?"

Her gaze came back to him. She smiled feebly. "Wondering whether you were coming and worrying over Robbie's present."

"Robbie's present! That's nothing to worry over. We'II go together and choose one tomorrow. I'll have time."

"Time!" She straightened up bravely, the way she had rehearsed the scene so often in her imagination. "Then it's true. You won't be here for Christmas? You're sailing?"

Her knowledge of his doings was uncanny. He came a step nearer, but she backed away. He realised her fear lest he should touch her. For a moment he was offended. Then, "My orders came today. How did you know? It was what I came to tell you."

"How did I know!" She laughed unsteadily. "How does one know anything? The heart tells one things sometimes. You'll be busy tomorrow—so many other things to think about. Robbie's present doesn't matter. It's growing late... Good-bye." He stood astonished at her abruptness. What had he done that she should be so anxious to rid herself of him? When he did not seem to see her proffered hand, but stared at her gloomily, her nerves broke. "Go. Why don't you go?" she cried fiercely. "You know you'll be happy."

"You want me to go?" he asked quietly. Had she heard her own voice, she would have given way to weeping. With her handkerchief pressed tightly against her lips, she nodded.

He turned slowly, looked back from the threshold for a sign of relenting and dragged his way haltingly down the stairs. In the hall beneath the mistletoe he paused to listen. He fancied he had heard the muttering of sobbing. So long as he paused he heard nothing; it was only when he began to move that again he thought he heard it. Having flung his coat about his shoulders, he eased his arm into the sleeve. This wasn't what he had come for—a very different ending!

And now the chance of the little house had arrived. Windows, chairs, tables, walls, we had all pledged ourselves to help her. He attempted to let himself out; the frontdoor refused to budge. He pulled, tugged and worked at the latch without avail.

"Shan't go. Shan't go. Shan't go," ticked the grandfather's clock excitedly. Then the usual thing happened, which always happened when the grandfather's clock got excited.

There was a horrible *whirr* of the spring running down; the weights dropped with a bang.

In the silence that followed he listened. She thought he had gone. There could be no mistake now; she was crying as if her heart would break.

The stairs creaked to warn her as he ascended. She could not have heard them, for when he stepped into the room she took no notice. She had sunk to the floor and lay with her face hidden in the cushions of the chair, with the gold light from the lamp spilling over her. For some moments he watched her—the shuddering rise and fall of her shoulders.

"You told me to go," he said. "The little house won't let me; it was always kind to us." And then, when she made no answer, "It's true. I've got my sailing orders. But it was you who told me to go."

She was listening now. He knew that, for the half-moon shoulders had ceased to shudder. The smell of Jacqueminot drew him to her. Bending over her, he stole one hand from beneath the buried face. "Do I need to go?"

And still there was no answer. It was then that the old grey parrot spoke. He had pretended to be sleeping. “What shall we talk about?” he whispered hoarsely; and, when an interval had elapsed, “Robbie?”

The little lady, who had needed to be loved, lifted up her tear-stained face and the wounded officer who had wanted rest, bent lower.

“I don't need to go,” he whispered. “I came to bring you Robbie's present. He told me what he wanted.”

THE END

www.ingramcontent.com/pod-product-compliance
Lightning Source LLC
LaVergne TN
LVHW101930220826
846093LV00009B/414

* 9 7 8 9 3 5 4 7 8 7 1 5 7 *